It's All Gumbo to Me
Examining our world through the metaphor of Gumbo

Cyrus Marcellus Ellis, PhD

Editor: Cyrus Marcellus Ellis, PhD
Series Editor: Cyrus Marcellus Ellis, PhD
Assistant Editor/Reviewer: Colleen Rock, MS
Consultant: Jill Renee Robinson, PhD
Supportive Consultant: Tracey Kim Snow, MA, CFT, LPC

Student Support Staff:
    Dreena Greenwood
    Lynea Fenderson
    Debra Baymon
    Lauren Osman
    Anita Brown
    Jennifer Thomas
    Jacqui Ross

Copyright © 2008 Cyrus Marcellus Ellis, PhD

All rights reserved. No part of the material protected by this copyright notice may be reproduced or utilized in any form or by any means, electronic or mechanical, including photocopying, recording, or by an information storage and retrieval system without written permission from the copyright owner.

To obtain permission to use material from this work, please submit a written request to Dr. Cyrus Marcellus Ellis, 1 University Parkway, University Park, Illinois 60466. You may also email a written request to ellisprofessionalservices@yahoo.com. Fees may apply.

Ellis, PhD, Cyrus Marcellus
    Its All Gumbo to Me: Examining our world through the metaphor of Gumbo/ Cyrus Marcellus Ellis, PhD

Includes Additional readings and an extra essay.
ISBN 978-0-6151-9250-5
1.   Its All Gumbo to Me. I. Ellis, Cyrus II. Title

Printed in the United States of America

Dedicated to those who lifted up prayers since the Middle Passage

For
Courtney Lynn "Courtneylazie" Ellis
&
Morgan Cristina "Cheesy" Ellis

For their ancestry
&
In Memory of their Grandfather

Mr. Lionel A. Ellis, Sr.
"The Alka Saltzer"

Contents
Preface p.6

Chapter 1.
The Gumbo Pot and the Roux p. 12
Chapter 2.
The Trinity: Hope, Meaning, Spirit p. 20

Chapter 3.
Nature p. 32
Chapter 4.
Perception v. Apperception p. 36

Chapter 5.
History p.39
Chapter 6.
The Rice p. 43

Epilogue p. 45

Additional Reading p. 47

Langiape p. 48

Preface

For such a long time I have been contemplating the content of this book. I have made the life of the mind my calling since 1997 when I began my doctoral studies. This book is the beginning of a series of work that will examine the human condition through the use of a metaphor-the metaphor of "Gumbo".

What brought this book together is the idea that everything that occurs in this world impacts everything else in the world. It is not a new idea by any stretch of the imagination; however, what makes this book different is that it is written for all people- students, parents, professors, teachers and everyday people. The lesson contained in each volume is that everything that we see, hear, have forgotten about, learned of and speak to is, in its basic sense, are ingredients in the gumbo.

The phrase, "Its All Gumbo to Me" refers to the results of good things and bad things occurring everyday to everyday people as they try to meet life on life's terms.

In my professional capacity as a counselor, counselor educator and social activist I have found that many of my clients, as well as everyone else, try to cope with the nature of their immediate world and the larger world that surrounds them. When clients struggle with their understanding the way of the world around them or their ability to get through difficult times, some degree of dysfunction can occur. While this can manifest itself into a variety of psychological issues, usually it lingers in our minds and can cause some trouble in how we relate to ourselves, others and our world.

While there are many people attempting to answer many questions concerning how people can live a better and more fulfilling life in spite of what happens to them, this book and this series attempts to have people understand society by recognizing how our lives, in conjunction with other people's lives, come together and mixes with a host of circumstances that yields a world of highs and lows-all through the understanding of a pot of gumbo.

Its All Gumbo to Me is a three volume set of writings concerning our lives and our society. Each volume will contain three books appropriately labeled Book 1, Book 2 and Book 3. The third book of each volume will signal the end of that volume. Each book for each volume contains societal concerns that impact our lives from our living rooms to our neighborhoods and extending out to our nation and the world.

This book opens with Chapter 1 which initiates the most important aspect of how this metaphor is a link to improving our ability to recognizing the best aspect of human existence which is our capacity to love. In chapter 1 we begin looking at how the roux of gumbo is like our capacity to have love for ourselves and for others.

The roux starts the gumbo. The roux will be used to explain how love (i.e. of self, for others, for life), like the roux, touches everything. The roux will be the vehicle for understanding how love makes a difference in what we do and how it touches all of our human spaces. As we cannot cook a meal without fire under the pot, fire will serve to represent the as the "heat of lives" or the -isms of life (i.e. racism, ableism, sexism, genderism, etc). These –isms represent the heat that is applied to our lives and I will explain how this heat can undermine our capacity to love and get along in our society. The meal of gumbo will be explained to illustrate the manner of how slaves created this dish as well as helping the reader learn about the metaphor and how it will be used throughout the series. Chapter 2 will introduce the basics of gumbo which include the "trinity" (i.e. onion, celery, and bell pepper) of ingredients and how these real ingredients serve as the link to human characteristics such as hope, meaning and spirit.

Chapter 3 is where we start adding the ingredients to our gumbo, the first ingredient that I add in is the ingredient of nature.

Nature is not understood to be trees, grass and rivers. Rather nature is understood to be an explanation of how there are forces that produce and control things around us. Additionally, the implicit and explicit nature of our society will be illuminated to show that all of the ingredients in our societal gumbo do not have to be seen for it to impact our lives.

Chapter 4 adds the ingredients of perception and apperception. These two ingredients serve as a means for people to know or for them to think they know how the world, and the people in it, operates. Chapter 5 adds the hearty ingredient of history. It can be said that everything has a connection to history and I always say that everything has a historical context. History is an ingredient, much like salt is to any dish, which is not seen but can be detected or lacking depending on one's tolerance for it. History, whether known or unknown, is a powerful ingredient in our society and it is a force to contend with in our world. The inability to recognize the depth and breadth of history in our world can hinder our ability to navigate through society. Chapter 6 explains the importance of the only dimensions of our gumbo that is not in the collective pot-the rice. Rice is used to explain the different generations of people that get exposed to the gumbo over time. Gumbo is seldom served over the same rice from previous days. The rice is usually made fresh each time gumbo is served. Likewise, every generation is a recipient of the constitution and concentration of the previous generation's gumbo. For some the taste is bitter, for others the taste may seem a bit sour, for others something may be missing, still some may say it needs additional items, some may say it is a bit strong for their taste. The rice is fine, but when it comes into contact with the gumbo, things can change. Chapter 6 ends with looking at how we can become "chefs" of our gumbo.

The book ends with the bridge to the next book in the collection of volume 1. Book 2 continues the metaphor of gumbo by continuing to add societal ingredients to the roux we have already started. Book 2 will address the impact of addiction and recovery, physical and emotional pain, the mediums of the media, education and race.

This text is proudly and humbly dedicated to the ancestors. One of my mentors, and I am thankful to have a few, once taught me that African American academics, economists, educators and such are answers to prayers. Prayers lifted up since the middle passage. While a doctoral student at The University of Virginia (UVa) I learned that the remains of many slaves were buried on grounds and around Charlottesville, Virginia. It was relayed to me that we, African American students at UVa (this is a traditional way of writing my alma mater's acronym), need to recognize that our ancestors are lying on their backs looking up at us and what we are doing. To their presence and sacrifice I offer my work in honor of their lives and sacrifice.

There are two families of the American south to which I am a direct descendant. In the state of Mississippi are the Ellis'. In the state of Louisiana are the Tinsons. My father hails from Bay St. Louis, MS and my mother from Pointe-a-la-Hache, LA. My knowledge of my paternal and maternal grandfathers and grandmothers fuel my pride of self and my direction for life. I only met my maternal grandfather. My other grandparents died before I could know them. My maternal grandfather was named Oliver Tinson. His nickname was "Dove" or "Zay". He was a great man. He stood tall in the face of so much oppression and hatred. I learned of my paternal grandfather through many stories relayed to me by my relatives as well as the stories told to me by my father. His name was Albert Ellis, Sr. His nickname was "Big Boy". He was a tall man commanding great respect in a harsh and cruel Mississippi. Both of my grandfathers were farmers of the sea. Shrimpers and fisherman both, they harvested the bounty of the Louisiana bayous and the Gulf of Mexico. These men are the anchors of my ability to be hardheaded, persistent, to have courage and endure difficult times. To them, I am indebted.

My mother and father taught me a lot about gumbo. Mom made it and dad and the rest of us ate it. Watching her put the dish together was a great time for me. I did not know what she was doing but I knew she was doing it right. I watched her put items in the pot, the same pot she always used, with care and great skill. She never used measuring cups nor directions. I never saw her pull out a book and read a recipe. One day I asked her how do you know how much to put in the pot? She would always reply, "I just know, I have been doing this for years." In hindsight, I understand that her knowledge of how to make gumbo came with various attempts at getting right.

With every attempt to get the gumbo right, my mom recognized how the roux and other ingredients have to work together for the meal to come out right, likewise, the way in which we relate to each other in view of ingredients like white supremacy, class differences, gender differences, sexual differences and the like will also take time for us to figure out how they work together to make our world come out right-and it won't happen overnight. Honor and credit for laying the foundation for this book is to my mom, Augustine Ellis (her nickname is May-May).

My dad died in 1987 and is buried in Biloxi, Mississippi at the National Cemetery near an Air Force base. I visit his headstone often. I stand before it reading his name, rank, branch of service and dates of life over and over again. Tears usually come soon after I start reading it. I never used to think that I would talk to a stone when I was young, I always thought that was something that was a little odd-until it happened to me at the level it happened to me. I thank him for being my father. He was not my friend; I had a lot of friends. He was my father. He rode tall in the saddle and it was clear that he headed his household. He was not an abusive dad. He did not curse at his children and he did not do despicable things to us. He was a blue collar man who drove eighteen wheelers across the country. I spent many of my vacations with him on his truck and loved every minute of it. I would take that truck and the highways over Disneyland, Europe, amusement parks or anything else that existed. I miss him everyday. Honor and credit for the good aspects of me being a man and facing adversity with soul-force and integrity goes to my father, Lionel A. Ellis, Sr. (CB handle the "Alka Seltzer").

If you wonder why I included personal information in the preface, well, *it's all gumbo to me*. All of what I have written, and much more that I have not included for you to read, is part of my "seasoning" that goes into the pot (i.e. our world). Who I am and what has shaped me comes into contact with other people's seasoning. To move in a direction where we can begin to change the impact of the concentration of our world on each other we need to begin to be open with ourselves by investigating how we are shaped by the ingredients of our world. As chefs to our collective gumbo, we also need to learn that when we put too much of one ingredient in the pot that we may need to add other ingredients to our gumbo to even it out. Step one in this process begins with understanding ourselves and how humankind operates. No small task by any stretch of the imagination, but just like gumbo, we begin with the roux, add the trinity, monitor the heat and begin preparing the ingredients.

Let's start cooking...

Chapter 1

THE GUMBO POT & THE ROUX

One of the most interesting components of being an academic tasked with investigating the "ins" and "outs" of human existence is learning from the world that came before one's own time and consciousness. Our world possesses an abundance of works of art, selections of music, archives of literature and other forms of the liberal arts that have shaped the formation of people, nations, wars, and movements. While I may have some expertise on how human beings act toward themselves and others, there is so much more information available to the one who seeks it out that it becomes an exciting endeavor to be tasked with continually growing and seeking out how to help mankind grow and become more connected with each other.

It may be difficult for some to see the world we live in as a big pot sitting on a stove. For many of us it is quite normal to see pots and pans on the stove. As a child, it was quite normal to see a stove top covered with pots and pans simmering and bubbling with goodness. Many a Sunday afternoon was spent in anticipation of my plate being filled with the goodies of what those pots held. Although gumbo as a meal may not be something many are familiar with, most of us like to eat, so the metaphor of a gumbo pot ought to work for all of us.

From the history of the African slave in America, the meal of gumbo emerged. The name gumbo comes from a variety of places. Gumbo received its name from the word KIGOMBO meaning "okra". The word gumbo in Gullah means okra and many gumbo makers use okra as the central ingredient. While some may consider gumbo needing okra, other variations of gumbo leave okra out and instead just begin with the use of the trinity (onion, celery and bell pepper). When Africans first began arriving to Louisiana and other places throughout America, they brought with them this dish. After years of additional influence from the Spanish, the French and other mixes of slaves coming into the region, this dish became how we understand gumbo to be today. Once the preparer began the gumbo with the trinity, the meal could be made with meats, seafood or whatever else was available. Once the trinity began the dish, there were no hard and fast rules about how gumbo could be made.

We need to take pause at this point and I need to make an intentional point about this revelation concerning gumbo. Dr. Martin Luther King said once that we need to recognize that we are beholden to much of the world before we leave our homes every morning. We get our coffee, chocolate, sponges from people all over the world. Gumbo is a meal that many people enjoy when they are traveling the American south, but I wonder if anyone who enjoys gumbo recognizes the historical significance of the meal.

I see gumbo as a physical representation of how communities of people were able to survive in a harsh and unforgiving environment. It called for someone to have a pot and a few ingredients such as celery, onions and bell peppers. But that, by itself, was not enough. Someone had some fish or someone had some okra and someone had some shrimps or crabs. People came together in community to fellowship and survive. As individuals there was not enough for one to eat, but together there was enough for everyone. The gumbo pot and its contents serve as a means to understand the need to create communities through grass roots activities so people can better relate to themselves, others and the world around them.

The Gumbo Pot is Our World

I see the gumbo pot as our world. Ironically growing up as a child I was influenced early in my life by "the Great American Melting Pot" as portrayed in School House Rock cartoons on Saturday morning. They too put all of us in a pot and gave the impression that we all are in this together. Perhaps the producers of the cartoon had noble ideas in their concept, but they were a little light on the day to day reality of many people. The gumbo pot, I feel, is the proper starting point for our look into our world.

As I have said, when I make the statement *It's All Gumbo to Me* I am really referring to the world that we live in or the "gumbo pot" and what happens when you have a variety of events of life (i.e. ingredients) interacting with each other. We only have one world and so we only have one gumbo pot and we are all in it together-whether we like it or not. When I read of, see or hear of issues in and around the world I typically respond with its all gumbo to me. That response is not to sound callous or insensitive, but it is said to denote that good and bad things happen in our world. We may be saddened or disgusted by them but they do happen.

To create a collective gumbo that is palatable for all of us, we need to learn how to address the myriad of issues that face us as individuals that impede us from being active participants of changing our conditions. It's All Gumbo to Me refers to the need to be good cultural "chefs" by beginning to become active participants in constructing a world that is rich for human dignity, human acceptance and human worth.

The Roux

With a little oil and a little flour, you can make the roux. I don't know how others like their roux, but I like mine a little clear and soup-ish. Some like the roux a little dark and thick. The roux of gumbo is a very important part of how the gumbo will taste. Likewise, the roux serves as a metaphor for how our sense of love for ourselves and humanity touches everything in our lives and in our communities. Not only must we begin to examine the depth and breadth of our capacity to love ourselves and those around us, we must also be aware of what happens when our love is in short supply. Likewise, we must also be aware of how our love is affected by the heat under the pot. The greater the heat under the pot, the greater chance we have to scorch the roux which is symbolic of tainting everything or everyone in the pot.

Some time ago I was spending some time with a friend from high school. This friend of mine turned out to be my guardian angel because he rescued me from along side the highway in New Orleans after I was involved in a nine car collision with me being the number five car. I was on my way to meet him and some friends for lunch. I had a hankering for some gumbo (no surprise there). The accident occurred before I had a chance to get some gumbo, so as my friend rescued me and took me to the hospital he and another great friend from high school put me up over the next few days. On my last day before I was to fly home, my friend knew how much I wanted to have some gumbo and decided to make me and his family a pot before I left. He was so gracious to do so for me and I thanked him constantly. While he was making the gumbo he had the fire up a little too high and the roux became scorched. He did not know if he should throw it out or keep it; he decided to keep it. Although I enjoyed it immensely, you could taste the scorched roux and it was present in the rice, sausage, shrimp and chicken. As this is not a negative commentary on my very good friend it is, however, a commentary fit for my analogy. The roux of the gumbo, when tempered correctly, increases the palatability of the gumbo. When there is too much heat applied and the chef loses awareness to how much heat is being applied, the roux can get scorched.

Love is our roux. Love is an ingredient that is in short supply in and around the world today. Love as an ingredient in our collective gumbo is reflective of love of self, others and the world around us. Love of self involves an examination of who we really are. Love is rooted in our faith; it touches our intuitive sense of character and it feeds our strength of heart. Love is the ingredient that allows all of us to have compassion for ourselves and others, love allows us to have the power of forgiveness for ourselves and others, love allows us to be patient with ourselves & others and love allows us to recognize the beauty in ourselves and in others.

Love allows us to contend with the negative dimensions of the world we live in. This ingredient in our gumbo allows us to persevere through the impact of murders, assaults, racism, poverty, fear, addiction, sickness, police abuses, corporate abuses, government abuses and death. Love or the lack thereof impacts everything in the pot. Our sense of love will impact the way we hear requests for help, the need for personal involvement with suffering people, the ability we have to connect with oppressed people, how we create avenues of self improvement for those seeking a reconciliation of the soul through work and dignity. Our sense of love will touch the way we see crime and punishment. Our sense of love for ourselves and others will touch the range of our ability to be patient, be at peace and preserve our soul.

Humanistic love for each other is a dimension of life that is complicated when heat is applied. In an age where everyday people are being pinched between corporate powers that are out of control; political structures not representing the needs of the working class or the working poor and economic division tearing apart the middle class it may not be hard to see how love is in short supply.

Love is an ingredient that needs to be continuously added to our gumbo to lessen the bitterness of individualism and fear of the unknown. Current debates on immigration, war, and poverty are examples of the heat being applied and its results of that heat are visible on our sense of love and compassion that used to be the hallmark of a nation that was heralded for providing an opportunity for those willing to make hard work and determination their posture. Rather than providing for a foundation of dignity and respect for some of the world's poorest people to gain access to America and a chance at gaining a personal sense of dignity, we find ourselves caught up in the debate over who stays and who goes while at the same time there are corporations, who profit on the backs of people caught in the immigration crossfire, going unpunished for their continued abuse of people caught in the vulnerable position of needing any employment for the basic necessities of life.

Increasing the amount of love that we show for our fellow man, woman and child does not eliminate America nor its citizens, in fact, it may allow for America to critically fulfill its marketed place in the world as a land of opportunity. Humanistic love added to the gumbo allows for policies to be created in support of people's dignity as well as providing for a variety of approaches to self empowerment, self-efficacy and self-worth. It may sound like an old church hymn (because it is), but adding and continually monitoring the ingredient of love can move mountains, adding love can increase our love of all humanity, love can calm the seas of despair, slow hatred and intolerance, and lastly increasing love can save us from the shadows of our past.

The Heat

All fine cooking involves heat. Usually it is the heat from the fire, stove, or various types of ovens that gets the meal going. Under the gumbo pot is usually a nice fire that heats everything up and gets the roux and all the other ingredients mixing together nicely. My mom always said to me that you have to watch the fire under the pot. If the fire is too high you can scorch the roux and that "bad" taste will be throughout the gumbo. It will taint the shrimp, sausage, onion and everything else. She said that a good cook keeps their eye on the fire.

I use this example as a means to explain the heat of our world. It is not the sun nor is it global warming, for the purpose of this commentary the heat I am referring to is our need to pay attention to the heat caused by the –ism's of our world. I am referring to rac-ism, abel-ism (that which relates to disabilities), gender-ism, class-ism, heterosex-ism, and "broke-ism" (my slang for the impact of poverty).

Our society has a history, as all nations do, that combines the best of the human spirit and the sadness of how mankind can turn on each other. American history has within it a context of glory and sadness, justice and injustice, valor and treachery. What is often overlooked when our world is bubbling around in the gumbo pot is the source that provokes it. The fire under our pot is characteristic of the nature of racism, genderism, classism, heterosexism and brokeism on our society and the daily lived experience of people on the negative side of these issues. The heat of our world is not a simplistic entity; it has within it a certain kind of nature that makes it potentially dangerous.

The word **nature** defined refers to the forces that produce and control… this word has serious qualitative meaning in our society. When it comes to all of the –ism's in our world, the nature of the –ism's is most relevant. What produces the thought process that one color, one gender, one side of town or one type of car determines superior or inferior status? The nature of our heat source, those who produce and control it, create policies that can undermine humanistic value and moral individualism impacting the way we act and relate to self, others and the world around us. More will be said about the qualitative aspect of nature in chapter three.

W.E.B. DuBois wrote about this in his historic book *The Souls of Black Folk* (1903). He wrote, "What does it feel like to be a problem?"(p. 7). The question raised by DuBois is like asking what does it feel like to live inside of an –ism (i.e. racism, sexism, genderism, ageism, ableism, etc). There are a myriad of issues faced by individuals who live inside of a world where their morality, loyalty, patriotism, faith and fidelity are called into question by their very presence in the fabric of this nation. These are some of the items that get called into question when the heat rises. The answer to DuBois' question of what it feels like to be a problem is somewhat unanswerable. DuBois' answer of what it feels like to be a problem is that those of us who live with this kind of heat tend not to respond, we seldom say a word.

DuBois did one more thing for us; he understood our culture not by race, believe it or not, but by how our society is affected by the heat concerning our ability to mix with each other, it is something that we have been fighting over since the nation began. DuBois' understanding of the heat of our culture, as stated in 1903 was said this way…

"In the civilized life of to-day the contact of men and their relations to each other fall in a few main lines of action and communication; there is first physical proximity of homes and dwelling places. . .[second] there are economic relations…[which means] the production of wealth, the meeting of wants…[third] there are political relations…[that is to say] the cooperation in social control…laying and paying the burden of taxation…[fourth] there are the less tangible but highly important forms of intellectual contact and commerce…[which is] the interchange of ideas through conversation and conference [in common places]".

When the heat of our world rises, the aforementioned areas tend to break down and that turns up the heat on all of us and it scorches our ability to relate well to ourselves, to relate to one another and to institutions outside of our homes and communities. It provokes, what Dr. Cornel West calls, closed ranks mentality within and between the races which does little to fight off the fear and despair of everyday people of all races and abilities attempting to get their needs met.

Good social chefs will keep their eye on the heat so that it does not have opportunity to scorch the ingredients inside the pot. As we understand the gumbo pot and the roux in combination as a metaphor for the world we live in, we also recognize that we must monitor the nature of the heat otherwise it has the capacity to harm all of us who attempt to make change and positively impact our environment.

Let's keep cooking...

Chapter 2

"The Trinity"
Hope, Meaning, Spirit

In the gumbo tradition the trinity is considered onions, celery and bell peppers. I remember watching my mom and relatives prepare gumbo. It always began with getting the gumbo pot (we tend to use the same pot routinely to make gumbo so that the flavor of the gumbo is consistent) that familiar butcher knife and those vegetables from the bottom drawer of the refrigerator. Just seeing that pot on the stove meant that a very tasty meal was not far away.

In the Christian tradition, the trinity involves God the Father, His Son Jesus and the Holy Spirit. Each plays an important role in the Christian tradition to guide the heart, mind and soul of the Christian. Likewise the trinity for regenerating our world involves the trinity of hope, meaning and spirit. Each of these ingredients, when combined, has the capacity to positively influence the value and substance of our homes, communities, and world.

Hope

I don't know where the world would be if people did not have hope. I remember the "in-home" lessons taught to me by mom and dad concerning hope for the future. I remember the on-the-block prophecy of how one day we (African Americans) will rise up and claim our place within society in sports, music, politics and finances. In church, the Catholic ideology always spoke of the hope for the future because of the sacrifices of Jesus and the example of his apostles. As I grew older and became part of the Christian tradition of non-denominational churches, preachers and elders would speak of our hope through having faith that God will deliver what he promised and that is how we have hope for our souls and for others as well.

The good book says that faith is the substance of things hoped for, the evidence of things not seen (Hebrews 11:1). Hope is a key ingredient in the trinity of our world because hope (as it is constituted by ample supplies of faith) is the world's "crystal ball" for all that is possible for tomorrow. Hope allows the most oppressed, stressed and cut off individual or individuals to still see enormous possibilities for a better day.

How does one increase the ability of a people to have hope (No matter what the answer is, it is a very difficult task)? What I have deduced from a substantive review of my work in social services and through academic study is that hope is possible if you have a few key ingredients. Hope is made up of (a) burying our past baggage, (b) leaning on something that you may not be able to see (c) preparing the self & preparing others, and (d) being altruistic.

Burying our past baggage refers to the ability each of us have to put what belongs in the grave yard *in* the grave yard and leaving it buried. This is not a statement that is equal to the phrase, "get over it" or "just let it go." The latter phrases, in my opinion, trivialize the degree of human suffering that can go on in the heart and mind of people. What I mean by the statement of letting things die is equal to what many of us call the mourning process or the stages of grief. You see, mourning is a process, which means the person who is in mourning is engaged in a particular manner of coming into touch with the internal struggle of losing someone or something. It is a difficult process to go through when you experience a great personal loss. I know this from my practice and from personal experience. To let some things die, as it is asserted here, is to provide insight into how our hope is increased or diminished by the need to work through our baggage that is unfinished and incomplete and not prepared to be buried. It is, I think, an accurate analogy to use because we call our cemeteries a final resting place. Bodies are prepared in one place and made ready for public viewing in many cases, and then placed in their final resting place. Our unfinished business is usually never completely prepared for our historical cemetery.

We keep it alive and whether we know it or not we use the past, often at our personal disadvantage. To have greater degrees of hope requires each of us to have a psychological funeral.

Leaning on something that you may not be able to see refers to a spiritual song that was taught to me and that I sing from time to time. Leaning on something that you may not be able to see also refers to a recovery concept that I have seen in action over the course of seventeen years of working with people working to recover from drugs and alcohol. In the twelve step tradition step one is realizing that an individual is powerless over alcohol. That is a very hard but necessary step. Many people trying to recover have a difficult time with admitting to a state of powerlessness. Often their road of addiction is dark and dangerous and if they survive they think that their survival was based upon their strength to overcome great hardships, so they should be able to overcome their dependence on alcohol. In the twelve step tradition (and I don't endorse this as the only way to work a recovery program) step one takes some time because step two, recognizing a higher power, is the leaning step for me.

Although I have not had a problem with drugs or alcohol, I am in recovery. I am in recovery from pretty women, family problems, relationship problems, educational problems, vocational problems, money problems, automobile problems, money problems (did I say that already), promotion on the job problems, health problems, all kind of problems. Each issue as well as all of my issues combined can provoke me to get to a point where I just don't care and where I want to run away and cut all ties to them = losing hope. Like many of us, I lose hope that I can get to the other side of difficult times. That is where I must learn to lean. I must begin to lean on what works. What works is that I work *it* (a recovery phrase) every day. What works is that I lean on something greater than my finite ability to reason, judge and comprehend. What works is that I sustain my ability to do what is necessary (legitimately and healthy) to get through the next minute, hour or day. My view of humanity is that *we are all in recovery* and it is our recovery plan that is a part of the nature of hope. I must make my meetings (AA, NA, OA, GA, synagogue, mass, worship service, meditation time, personal time, etc), I must remember what sets me off and work hard to put some distance between me and the things that can sink my hope, I may need people in my life who work to help me see a different reality than I am able to see-and they don't always need to be friendly about it and I need to learn to respond rather than react while I work on gaining insight into who I am and what makes me better or worse. No small task, but perhaps that is why, in recovery, we say and try to live *one day at a time*.

Preparing the self and preparing others refers to the use of your time for self development and the time you take to connect with others. As a trained career counselor I hear many stories from young and old about what they want to do or wanted to do with their lives, respectively. Over the course of an individual's life, time is spent on worthy and perhaps not so worthy endeavors. Hope is an outcome for people who have spent a great deal of their time in a particular manner where they feel that a return on their investment of time in self preparation and the amount of time given to others is likely to occur. Hope, then, is in great amounts or in lesser amounts depending on the return of your investment of time over the course of your life.

Time is one thing that is spent and gone forever. For example, we cannot get back the Monday we had five years ago at 7 p.m. In my work of counseling people attempting recovery, the issue of time has always been a central issue. Sometimes clients would not be able to concretely tap into the concept of time and others would speak about the future while implying the need to compress present time because of lost time. As a professional counselor who worked with the chronic addiction population, many saw that their years of active addiction as wasted time that cannot be recovered. Clients who come out of their addiction, as well as those who come out of any emotionally debilitating or chronic condition that may provoke a withdrawal from social conditions, possess a strong need to make up for lost time. It is a feeling that people have, due in part to the concrete reality that their time left on this planet is growing shorter. Although people may say that they hope life can turn out the way they want, the need for their time to be profitable may profitable may inhibit the ability to have hope.

To increase the amount of hope that one can have when time is finite is to recognize that one's time is measured more by intensity and focus than by years. One famous existential question that is always asked is who lives a greater life-a man with one year to live or a man who lives for 100 years? It is an interesting question. On the one hand, a man who knows his time will end and copes adaptively can have the richest and most vibrant life possible. On the other hand a person that lives for 100 years has wisdom, life experience and the time to recover from early mistakes, but like the bible teaches, buries his talents and never uses them. Our investment of time provide for hope because we store up our future desires with action and works that can have a return in our future.

Lastly, being altruistic refers to doing acts of goodness for the sake of doing good. Certainly it is a value statement on my part to say that true hope is dependent upon all of the above issues if and only if our motives are just and good. I can own that piece, but it is important to recognize that my value-laden statement is not without some validation from eastern cultures, tribal cultures and even some famous theorists. My Native American brothers and sisters understand this through the concept of harmony. Their construct of harmony involves a concrete connection with all living things which are inclusive of the elements, plant life, rivers, mountains, stars, and clouds. To be harmonious with all that surrounds you requires a certain kind of attitude (i.e. posture) on the part of a person. Abraham Maslow, the great humanistic psychologist, recognized a person is in balance or in a state of homeostasis, when his body (physical needs), personal safety, sense of love and belonging and true self esteem are free from deficits or unfinished business. Maslow used the concept of homeostasis to teach human beings that we must consciously address all areas of our lives if we expect to be balanced.

It is my contention that our ability to have hope is a matter of our putting to rest our past, leaning on something that is outside of our selves, and preparing our selves and others as long as they are all wrapped up in altruistic motives and actions.

Meaning

There is no greater quest for many on this planet than to have lived and have our life mean something. Many people struggle with the desire to leave a footprint on the world *especially* when they become conscious of the fact that they will leave this planet one day. We want our lives to have meaning. Many want our time on this planet to count for something. We want the gifts of our lives (I believe we all have gifts) to be a known and have it count towards our legacy.

I have been asked by many students, colleagues and friends about why I became a professor. I have been asked about why I went through all the challenges of higher education as well as spending 20 years in the U.S. Army. Why? When it came to the issue of my education, my answer always involved the need to help people and be like my professors from college. I put a lot of meaning into what I saw in them. As an undergraduate student my professors had prestigious doctoral degrees and they wrote books. I remember wanting to be like Dr. Law, Dr. Simpkins and Dr. Murphy. I remember daydreaming about how much meaning my life would have if I could obtain what they had. In graduate school my model of perfect professorship was Dr. DeEsch. Wow! To be like him would propel me to heights of meaning I never knew were possible. When it cam to the issue of my military service, as a soldier turned officer through ROTC I thought that becoming a leader (i.e. sergeant or officer) commander and then a full Colonel, I thought that would make me have all the meaning I desired. What was funny is that once I achieved some of these things, I still did not obtain the meaning I was looking for.

Meaning is something that is, believe it or not, not granted solely by outside achievements. Meaning is a bit more complicated than that. *Meaning is a complex product consisting of humanity and relationships wrapped in patience.* Meaning serves our gumbo because it is the catalyst to work on our attention and our activities in building relationships through a real tangible bond with others that acknowledges their right to live. The glue that holds this together is the need for us to utilize patience in substantive amounts whenever possible. Patience is the wrapping that holds the ingredients of meaning because patience allows for life to unfold when things are not as clear as they could be.

There are many sayings in human existence that speak to the need for people to have greater degrees of patience. Patience allows for wisdom. The good book teaches that when we are children we speak as children, act as children and think as children. It also teaches that when we grow up we are to put away childish things. I have always understood this lesson to mean that our ways of thinking, acting and feeling that makes us unique (which many counselor educators and psychologists may call our personality) ought to change to a more mature manner of speaking, acting and thinking. Lacking patience is potentially devastating for our social, emotional, physical and mental development. In simple terms, we want our young to grow up and become patient so that things that tend to happen to us (puppy love, first real love, relationships, jobs and responsibilities) can be addressed at a rate where they are best able to handle them. I often use the phrase "not done cookin' yet" to describe this phenomenon. Patience allows for things to be revealed to us by serving as a reminder that there are times to wait on some things while we maintain attention to how we are relating to ourselves, other people and the world around us.

Ending the story concerning my own meaning, I found out that it wasn't the rank nor was it the college degree that made those things special; it was the relationships that I developed over those years that provided meaning for me. It was meeting and getting to know soldiers from across the country in all kinds of capacities. I wish I had the time to bore you with my military stories, but I must move on. Going through graduate school I met some incredible people whom I have shared many experiences with. My mentor as a professor is at Rider University (Jesse DeEsch). My pseudo father (a man I love very much) is at The University of Virginia (Dr. Robert H. Pate, Jr.). It is the attention to these relationships, as well as the experience of maturing and working with people attempting recovery from drugs and alcohol, that supplied the meaning that I was looking for. I only wish I was more patient while waiting for it. One thing that is for sure, even though I, and many others, are not as patient as we want to be, some things will only happen when it is time. Our impatient posture cannot change that.

The analogy is set and so is the foundation of our gumbo. Our trinity and our responses to the world around us are in the pot. As good chefs (that is to say good members of our society) we now can begin to sample our gumbo and add what is necessary to make it palatable. Likewise, if we want our communities as well as our world to be better we need to monitor what is going on with us, others and social institutions and adjust it as necessary so that people can experience their right to exist while working to get along with one another.

Spirit

There may be no more an important issue for humankind than to try and define what being spiritual means and then try and develop a sense of spirituality in all of humankind. The word "spirit" automatically conjures up a variety of definitions and subjective constructs for each of us. I will not make any foolish attempts to define spirituality for you. I will, however, speak to the role it has within our world to provide balance, self-regulation and personal peace of mind for all of humankind.

I am a religious man in the Christian tradition. I grew up Catholic, went to Catholic school for nine years. I changed the direction of my faith and followed a Christian tradition based on the Holy Bible. I have traveled and have become aware of other means of religious faith. I have studied religion and other faith based practices in existence in the United States and around the world and have yet to find a constant definition of what it means to be a spiritual person. Greater than my quasi search for what it means to be spiritual, I have also uncovered the dilemma of how it is said to work in people and how it is used in the lives of people.

I have also looked at races of people such as Asians, Indigenous People of North America and tribal people from around the world and I tried to learn how they view their overall sense of spirit. It is an interesting journey to take when trying to answer the question on what is spirit, what does it mean to be spiritual and how does it work.

There are many writers who have the ability to write about spiritual things better than I. In fact, there are many books on the market defining or attempting to define religion, spirituality and so forth to anyone willing to read about it. The reason this ingredient is in the trinity is because of the common theme that I have discovered from my travels and my study into this phenomenon. The theme that I discovered is what underscores the need for this ingredient to be in the trinity. The one thing that emerged from my travels and my study was that spirit was a non-man made *connection* to the self.

Dr. Cornel West, in his book *Race Matters*, speaks to the decay of the black tradition that produced so many greats in African American history such as Fannie Lou Hamer, Carter G. Woodson, W.E.B. DuBois to name a few because of a decline of a connection to who we were as a people. He speaks of the black community being under siege from supremacist ideology threatening the intellectual capacity of a people as well as market culture values of buying and selling each other through sports and entertainment as well as the quest for the almighty dollar robbing people of their overall connection to powerful traditions of self-regulation, self-reliance and community. African

Americans are not the only one's under attack from these forces, American youth of all ages and races feel the impact of the MTV, BET, and other cable stations & internet market places of advertised values of sex, greed, and selfish individualism. Even our TV churches and some local churches have turned away from the straight and narrow and formed allegiances to follow a gospel of riches and extravagance that has me think of their actions as a *zeitgeist* gospel, not one of spiritual enrichment and brotherly service.

A non-man made connection defining one's spirit emerged because it appeared to me that the spiritual actions of humanity were never intended to be bought or sold. The Indigenous People of North America regard their spirituality as a connection of body, mind and soul. They view spirit, much like Asians and other tribal people, as being present in everything. They see their overall "health" coming from being connected to the world that *they are a part of not in rule over.* In my 17 years in treating people attempting to recover from drugs and alcohol, the 12 step programs operate off of similar principles of connecting to something other than self. Christians are taught of the God and His Son Jesus who came here to free them from their sins. The Christian tradition talks of building a relationship with His Son so that one can know God. The Christian tradition speaks to the need to make a connection and learn how to lean on Jesus. When traveling in Nepal I discovered a rich and spiritual people living within a spiritual context without clear rules of churches and religious dogma. It seemed that their faith came from the heart (which is why they may give the greeting Namaste). They had a strong connection to something outside of themselves.

A non-man made connection is a source of strength because it operates outside of the market culture values spoken of by Dr. West and it insulates the internal reaches of individuals. A non-man made connection is there to serve everyone because it provides for a sense of peace in troubling times and situations, it serves to regulate one's choices between that which could be healthy and those choices which could provoke negative actions, it allows for reflection (which some call meditation or prayer or fasting) and it may also provide us with an opportunity to gain greater appreciation for what we have versus what we still want. The only thing that can prevent the non-man made connection from being useful is adopting a man-made connection.

Man made connections is born in someone else's ideals that do not stand up when heat is applied. An example of this is, for me, the justice system. Our ideology of America says that justice is blind. We recognize that the law ought to treat everyone the same without passion or prejudice. Some may go as far as to recognize that everyone in America can get a fair trial-still! Well, I believe in the ideology more than the people who must act upon it. I am connected to the fact that justice will be done, but it may not happen here on Earth. I understand that, even in Jesus' time, that what was true was not always accepted and that those who were innocent often were harmed. When injustice is before me, my connection to justice does not rest with the prosecutor or defense attorney or in the jury. Certainly, these people are entrusted with a great responsibility, but after I have done what I can do, I must give it up to something higher than me.

This is the great challenge for so many of us, to trust our fate to an entity we might not truly believe in or truly understand. As a result, we begin to trust in things that are fleeting-jobs, cars, houses, money, social fame and the like. As it is in addiction recovery before anyone took their first step they hit rock bottom. Which usually means everything that they were using to sustain their addict lifestyle is gone, there is nothing left and they are in a position of emotional, and usually, physical turmoil and they realize that the promise of the bottle or drug cannot support them anymore. Their journey usually begins after that with learning how to connect with their life so the shadows of their past can be addressed one day at a time. Thus, the building of a non-man made connection. The person in recovery sees the problems of life again, but they respond differently and they do not fall prey to the ways of old. Such is the case for all of us when we have developed a non-man made connection. We begin to see our world in a different light. We can slow down and address the other ingredients in such a way that allows the room for understanding and patience. We now have regained our balance; we are self-regulated and can gain a sense of personal peace.

Our gumbo is now prepared and ready for other ingredients to be added. As this is a volume series, there are many topics (ingredients) that can be added to illuminate the culture of our world. This volume begins the investigation by adding cultural ingredients such as *nature, perception v. apperception, history* and most important to good gumbo, *the rice.*

Let's add the ingredients...

Chapter 3

Nature

Mother Nature was a term I first became familiar with because of a 70's T.V. commercial for some butter company. As a child I thought Mother Nature was the woman in charge of the rain, sleet, snow, rivers, mountains, wind etc. Well I am glad I began to know better than that from going to school and learning things in science class. What is interesting about the title "Mother Nature" is what it implies to me now that I have learned what the word nature means. As stated earlier, nature refers to "the forces that produce and control…" The term Mother Nature could easily mean, then, that there is a person (in this case a woman) who individually determines the manner of weather we receive on earth. The farmer that needs rain, the mountains that need snow, etc comes from "mom" and we are at her discretion. I don't mind the fable, but in terms of our collective gumbo, the critical explanation of the term nature is an important ingredient to consider when attempting creating a world tolerable for all.

The ingredient of nature, as it relates to our world, is an important one. It is also a dimension of life that is known in various circles by the phrase, "it is not what you know but who you know." A more pure form of this phrase is, "it is not who you know but who knows you."

We live in a society that has, what I have called, *Contradictory Rules of Engagement*. Contradictory Rules of Engagement refers to the inequitable impact of our nation's ideology on people of color, women and the poor. As a former soldier and Army officer it is difficult for me to separate myself from military examples and terminology. Soldiers exist under rules of engagement. Rules of Engagement (or ROE) critically dictate how military personnel are supposed to engage the enemy. Many service members are familiar with the phrase *do not fire until fired upon*. A phrase like that will come from the ROE briefed to the service members.

Our nation has an ideology of hard work, determination, and because we are all free people you have all you need to make it in America. The purported belief systems that we ought to have in our police officers, courts, private and public businesses, schools, churches and other cultural entities typically provide the ROE for our nation. Phrases such as, "stay in school," "just say no," "nose to the grindstone" and such provide a way of raising our young and teaching them about the 'right' or 'wrong' way to approach our society. Contradicting the aforementioned ideological positions and other worthy ideals is the dynamic of people and the nature of how things work. As nature is about the forces that produce and control, it is not hard to see how worthy ideals can become 'bumper stickers' only and not have any redeemable value when it comes time for people to "cash in" on the promises of the phrases. (Dr. King spoke of this during the march on Washington, if you have never read his speech-go get it and read it. If you read it before-please read it again.)

When we enter into any business, school, neighborhood, apartment building, the military, the music business, church environment or what have you, the nature of the environment surrounds and it is most important. Our bosses have people they listen to and those they do not. There are those who are in action behind the scenes who influence the action of people who have the position of authority. There are presidents of organizations who do not have as much power or influence as their executive directors. When I became commander of my Army unit, I had the position of authority and some additional authority, but the nature of my unit was also in the hands of others who made things happen on a daily basis. I had to learn *the* ROE of my unit if I were to be successful.

The reaction by many outside of Jena, Louisiana is an example of people not realizing the nature of the south, small southern towns, the legacy of slavery and Jim Crow, and black and white. The Jena Six case showed that the ideology of law and order is separate from the nature (forces that produce and control) of the law in Jena, Louisiana. From top to bottom, school officials, teachers, Christians, parents, the children, the police and the DA's office failed to address an issue that was staring them in the face for multiple years. The nature of that town was not to address racism, hatred and bigotry and call everyone to task. The nature of Jena, Louisiana showed itself and, somewhat necessarily, showed itself to the world. That town's DA showed himself to the world that he was the law and that justice, for everyone concerned, was not on his agenda. For those living outside of small town America and especially small town-racially divided America, these events seemed ridiculous. But there are many people in our society who recognize that you don't create discord with certain families, or you don't speak up at church because of who the pastor is, or you don't complain to a principal about one of his/her initiatives because of what could happen to you. It is not just in Louisiana, it is everywhere.

Often people say things like, "why don't people work harder to get ahead?", or others sometimes say, "I made it and nobody gave me anything," as a means to explain what people need to do in order to improve themselves. While self-determination and intestinal fortitude are necessary traits to possess for success, the aforementioned statements, and many like them illuminate the absence of awareness when it comes to the nature of things.

As a professor, I am the nature of my classroom. If I were an unethical person, I could produce a syllabus and set of classroom policies that could only make it possible for a few to pass my course no matter how smart my students are or how intelligent they may be. If I were to ever have a great deal of influence, I could also make it very difficult for students to appeal my class room policies because I may affect the nature of grievance committees and appeal panels.

Being aware of nature is instrumental to any "social chef". Nature works in our world in a variety of ways and all of us need to remain vigilant to what people are doing and the policies they are creating. If we want justice, better schools, better school policies and political and social reform, we need to have a critical look at who is responsible for reform by continually questioning the nature of those tasked with decision making and how they go about deciding courses of action.

Chapter 4

Perception v. Apperception

Perception is defined as, "the recognition and interpretation of stimuli based chiefly on memory" conversely apperception is defined as, "the process of understanding by which newly observed qualities of an object are related to past experience" (Webster's Collegiate Dictionary, 1993). What do we really know? How did we really get to know it? Is it live or is it a well produced copy on an exceptionally good tape that makes us think it is live (spoof on a 70's commercial)?

It may be a play on words or equally an argument over semantics, but I happen to think the two words above are important ingredients in the world we live in. In a world that is so diverse, how can we accurately perceive anything? Is that what we are actually doing? I strongly believe that we have within our collective gumbo too much of one ingredient-perception, and not enough realization that what are really 'tasting' is the other-apperception. For me apperception is like the food seasoning *Accent*. I never knew what it did but Mom always used it-I assumed it was like salt-an example of my apperception.

In our collective gumbo, whether we know it or not we are implicitly asked to make sense of a great many things, often times, without the benefit of full information. We assume that our news, education, friends and family, government officials and the like are not intentionally trying to mislead us when it comes to issues of civic and social importance.

Many people assume that the information they receive, as well as, the society they interact with is understood through their own perception. After all, a sound perception allows each individual the ability to discern the difference between fact and fiction. What is often overlooked is the fact many of us don't have an understanding of things that are foreign to our experience. Our experience is our perception. For many of us, we try to make sense of things or people in our society having never experienced before through apperception-using our past to make sense of new things in front of us.

National policies, school board policy, church policy, elementary school policy, believe it or not, operate more out of apperception than out of perception. It could be said that we all have perceptive qualities, and they would be right if and only if they mean that they can make sense of a "thing" because this "thing" that they are seeing or experiencing happened before with all of the same qualities and all of the same circumstances. That is the truest meaning of perception. Perceptive qualities involve the power of accurate recall of a past experience in order to accurately understand present day experiences. The memory you have of this phenomenon, to be accurate, must be inclusive of all of the past issues intact. When there is something new added to our experience it is a newly observed, and therefore, without any connection to our past experience.

The importance of these two words and their critical understanding cannot be overlooked in our collective gumbo. How can we learn to relate to each other unless we recognize the barriers to getting to know one another? As we seek to aid our collective gumbo, we need to guard against too much *perception* and seek to add in apperceptive qualities to make our collective gumbo better for everyone. The ability to recognize that we are attempting to relate with each other through the memories of our past ought to provoke all of us to increase our collective cooperation on meeting people by connecting with them from an intentional, equitable and level position. Dr. Martin Luther King, Jr. wrote about this very fact many years ago about race relations by saying

> "Like life, racial understanding is not
> something that we find but something that we must
> create. And so the ability of Negroes and whites to work

together, to understand each other, will not be found ready made; it must be created by the fact of contact."

Perceptive qualities, by definition, work against Dr. King's concept because it fails to allow for people to come together. Contact puts everyone in a position to confront each other and begin the process of forming bonds of care through dialogue and true human concern. When the heat rises in our collective gumbo you will find that the ability for people to get together and discuss their issues with each other is hampered by a refusal to see things from another's perspective because our perceptive qualities tend to take over. It is only possible to resolve interpersonal conflict when we recognize that we need to add apperceptive qualities into each of us so that every individual can recognize that their interactions may not be driven by the roux and the trinity, but by our own memories and our own assumptions.

Chapter 5

History

I have a beautiful 13 year old daughter who asks me from time to time to help her with her homework. Math, science and social studies are the subjects that she chooses to ask for my help. I say she chooses because her language arts classes are the territory for her mother. She likes the way her mom helps her with those subjects so that is not my territory. I usually have to regain my math abilities and my science abilities when she needs help with those subjects (sometimes it makes me wonder if I ever learned any of those things when I was young), but when it comes to social studies she approaches me with caution. Not because I yell or don't know the content, she approaches me with caution because she knows that I will begin to help her with what she is learning but I will always go into a story or three (more like ten) about what is not being included in what she is learning. She likes and hates that I do that to her at the same time.

History, as an ingredient to our collective gumbo, is critically important. Most history provides a record of what has occurred over time from a particular point of view, but it also includes a record of what humankind needs to free itself from in order to improve society at all levels. History is the map of our future-or at least I think so. An accurate record of our past is the mechanism to break the shackles that keep us and future generations in bondage. We all need an accurate view of history concerning the formation of this nation, which has to include the elimination of thousands and thousands of indigenous people; we need to accurately address the history of slavery in this nation and its lasting effects in American society regarding civil liberties and democratic inclusion; we need to address the historical context of men relating to women. Ultimately, we need to recognize that history has within it multiple dimensions of responses that fuel attitudes and dictate interactions among all of us.

History is not just a 'thing' that we study. For many people history is representative of their life and their family's life. As an example to my previous assertion, the history of slavery and the manner by which African Americans have been systematically oppressed has its historical roots in slavery from the 1700's and Willie Lynch. Willie Lynch's message to Virginia plantation owners in the 1700's can be credited for laying the historical foundation for a system of oppression of African Americans in the new world. Willie Lynch is reported as providing slave owners of the new world with a "sure-fire" way of keeping those Africans fighting among themselves for at least 300 years, perhaps thousands. His approach, tested on his plantations, were to keep these slaves fighting among themselves by telling white slave owners to mix with the slave women and create bi-racial children, to pit the old against the young, to pit men against women, and to make all slaves think that they can only trust you [the slave owner] and no one else. Sadly, we have been dancing to this tune for hundreds of years. As an example of this phenomena, Barrack Obama's quest for the Presidency is a noble one, but when people ask the question is he 'black' enough or can he blacks really get behind Obama, it flows from the historical path of being continually filtered through the "Willie's way". The press as well as opposing candidates and political pundits continually drum up the facts concerning his race, his bi-racial status and his living outside of mainstream "Black America" rather than the failed attempts of other politicians from providing a means of recompense for African Americans as well as all citizens.

There is not enough space to cover all the necessary, historical pieces that contribute to our collective gumbo. I will say that when we try to even out the 'taste' of our gumbo we better be prepared for the reactions some of us possess because history is shaped by our perception and that makes our ability to engage others difficult. History is also a powder keg of emotions sometimes ruled by who is considered to be right or considered to be wrong.

Dr. Cornel West warns that we need to address our historical amnesia. He says that when we begin to experience historical amnesia we begin to play games with our fame or glory. We tend to think that we are where we are by our own sense of self-determination and self-will. While the aforementioned characteristics are necessary they, by themselves, are not enough. At The University of Virginia there are many placards on grounds (we don't say campus) indicating burial sites of the remains of slaves owned by various families. The University of Virginia was founded by Thomas Jefferson-one of the architects of the new nation and of the institution of slavery. It was unique thing for me, as an African American, to walk around grounds and see those placards and look down to realize that my ancestry's remains are below my feet. It is a strange feeling to connect with the fact that I was attending this institution to gain its highest degree while my slave ancestry lies in graves unmarked all around me. One African American professor told me that if you truly want to make a connection with the history of the institution, think about the fact that your ancestry is lying on their backs looking up at you and then ask yourself if they would be proud of what you are doing?!

It is our history that created Black History Month, propelled MLK day, keeps the Confederate flag flying, it made Jackie Robinson a hero, sustains the Klu Klux Klan, created the Black Panthers, provoked wars, made Hank Aaron's home run race-related, made female astronauts special, created affirmative action, illuminated Nancy Pelosi's role, created the ACLU, created the NAACP, created the SCLC, made Clarence Thomas a hero or a sell out, provoked the need for women's awareness month, hampered the recovery of the Gulf Coast after Katrina, hampers Hillary Clinton's run for president, makes Black kids think that school is for white kids, and on and on and on.

History, as an ingredient in our collective gumbo, is quite substantive. It is a shaper of our policies and our values. Not recognizing the depth and breadth of our history continues to enslave us because it prevents us from facing the good, the bad and the ugly. It does not allow for us to make amends and move forward with a clear sense of where the pitfalls are that hinder us from being able to relate well to self, others and the world around us.

Chapter 6

The Rice

There is one last ingredient to good gumbo and it is probably the only ingredient that is outside of the pot and that is the rice. In the gumbo tradition, you may keep gumbo from night to night and continually serve it until it is gone. The rice, however, is not carried from day to day. The rice is made daily and the old gumbo (mom's always tasted better the second and third day-if it lasted) is poured out over it.

Rice serves as the metaphor for the generations. As gumbo is poured out over new rice, the world that we create is routinely 'ladled' out to a new generation. Every generation must, whether they like it or not, contend with the world that was created before their time. Each generation is created anew and receives on top of them the ingredients of the past which may not 'taste' as good as previous servings of our gumbo.

Each generation has to make a multitude of decisions impacting the course and direction of that generation. History has taught us that some generations made decisions about the new America or about aiding the Europeans in armed conflict and saving the world from tyranny, and some generations even made the decision to question their government and exercise their American freedoms to voice their displeasure of a government who appeared to turn a deaf ear to the citizenry during WWII. Tom Brokaw's book, *The Greatest Generation* is an account of a generation of men and women during the World War II era to go off to war, fill the factories, and endure rationing the nation's resources as well as to go off to fight and die in fields of battle all over the world. To them, which include members of my family, I give my eternal gratitude. That generation had to make a decision about the ingredients of their world and work together to make their collective gumbo better for future generations.

But I assert there are other great generations of men and women who boycotted buses, marched on Washington, demonstrated in Chicago and Kent State, burned their bra's, and organized to protect Black communities so that future generations can collectively create a world with the ingredients of freedom, respect, and community protection.

Intervening in our world today is as much about fixing our current situations as it is about creating a more endurable and substantive mixture for future generations.

I am reminded of a story I was told concerning the bus boycott of 1955-1956. An old Negro woman was walking and a cab driver pulled over and asked the old woman to please get in the cab. It was obvious to the cab driver that the old woman was having difficulty walking. The cab driver pleaded with this old woman for a time but the old lady refused. Before the cab driver could utter another plea to the old woman the woman looked at the cab driver and said to him, 'I am not walking just for me, I am walking for my children and my grandchildren." This is an example of one generation attending to the mixture of a previous generation when it recognized that the collective gumbo was not good and needed an increase in the ingredients of love, dignity, patience and faith.

It is up to each new generation to examine and address the collective gumbo being served so that future generations can receive a world that is tolerable for all. Each generation can leave a legacy for those who will be coming after them by being an active chef that examines the ingredients of their world and then work hard to provide leadership by impacting the quality of individual lives, communities and the world.

Epilogue

"Everybody can be great. Because anybody can serve. You don't have to have a college degree to serve. You don't have to make your subject and your verb agree to serve. You don't have to know about Plato and Aristotle to serve. You don't have to know Einstein's theory of relativity to serve. You don't have to know the second theory of thermodynamics in physics to serve. You only need a heart full of grace. A soul generated by love."

-The Reverend Dr. Martin Luther King, Jr.

The above quote from Dr. King underscores the reason for this book and subsequent volumes. We all are in this world together. That is an ideal that we cannot escape. Our world is shaped by the varying degrees of our participation at each level of our society. Dr. King's words of a time ago ring true today because of its love ethic. Love is the roux that touches everything in our world. The world has been blessed by those among us who display a myriad of actions based on their love for their fellow man.

Volume 1 book 1 provided us with the foundation of our gumbo. Book 2 will continue the metaphor of gumbo by adding societal ingredients to the roux and trinity already started in book 1. Book 2 will address the impact of addiction and recovery, physical and emotional pain, the mediums of society, new warriorship, education & race.

This text was designed to begin the dialogue of how everyone can be an active participant in preparing our world to be acceptable to as many people as possible. Dr. King's quote is designed to remind us as this book draws to a close that we all have a share in the way our world is constructed and how it is ladled out to current and future generations. We all can serve with what we have inside of us. We cannot allow the seasonings of darkness to overpower the ingredients of light. The foundation of our world-our roux (love) and trinity (our hope, meaning and spirit) make it possible for everyone and anyone to contribute significantly to the collective gumbo of our world.

This is how we become the chefs of our world. We become the chefs of our world by learning what makes a good collective gumbo. Good chefs learn and understand how ingredients work together to make a good gumbo for all. Good chefs take the time to ensure that all the necessary ingredients on hand and in good supply. As good chefs, we are careful and intentional as we monitor the heat under our mixture because too much heat can scorch and taint all the ingredients inside of the pot causing a bitter taste to form over everything contained in the pot. We are good chefs because we prepare our collective gumbo with love and respect, we guard against improperly adding ingredients or choosing ingredients that can harm the taste and utility of what is being created.

Additional reference books

Race Matters by Cornel West.
ISBN 0-8070-0972-5

The Words of Martin Luther King, Jr.
2nd Edition
ISBN 1-55704-483-x

Langiape

Concerning African American Males and Wellness

The literature concerning self-concept for African American adolescents reveal two key elements. First, research on African American self-concept began with color preference studies in the 1930's. Early research interpreted the choices African Americans made between white dolls and black dolls to infer positive or negative self-concept. The greater frequency that Black adolescents chose the white dolls over black dolls, the greater the inference was that the choice proved that Black people possessed a low self-concept. This research methodology negated the influence of an oppressive society and did not investigate the culture of African American people. Second, the research into Black self-concept changed in the 1960's with the rise of the "Black Power" movement. The Black Power movement was seen as the catalyst for the rise in Black self-concept. Additionally, the 1960's saw an increase in African American researchers investigating Black self-concept, which included the examination into the Black subculture. Self-concept scores for African Americans that matched or surpassed White Americans were interpreted as a result of the growing appreciation and knowledge of Black culture coursing through the African American middle class community.

The work on self-concept for African Americans also includes the examination of African American families. The key findings for examining the role the family has in self-concept development for urban African American adolescents are (a) Black self-concept possesses three dimensions interconnected and fastened to relationships with family, friends, and community, (b) economic hardship has a negative effect on the quality of familial relationships and (c) role models for urban youth include musicians, sports figures, and mothers.

The African American male confronts a plethora of external forces and conflicting internal messages. Understanding the areas that shape the self has the potential to assist an individual to avoid various *hidden dangers* located within our society. The focus of this commentary involves the examination of three areas possessing hidden dangers that African American men face (1) articulating the particular items involved in developing a healthy sense of self, and (2) the precarious posture of nihilism. These areas directly relate to the ability of African Americans to maintain overall wellness concerning themselves, other people and societal systems.

Crain and Bracken (1994) formalized the process of examining the self by combining the work of Shavelson, Stanton and Hubner (1976) and in so doing created a model of understanding the self by interlocking six identifiable domains (affect, social, physical, competence, academic, and family) that constitute a global self concept. Crain and Bracken's definition of the self is systematic according to identifiable and comprehensive responses involving an individual's achievements and failures in an assortment of environments, the way in which other people choose to respond to their actions, and the approach other persons take to mirror their actions and transmit their behaviors.

Consequently Crain and Bracken encapsulates the self, "as an organized response pattern that is acquired and maintained through an individual's actions upon and reactions to stimuli in various environmental contexts".

Understanding the self through Crain and Bracken's established point of reference generates some interesting questions when applying this construct to African Americans, 1) to what extent do socio-racial injustices factor into the African American male's response pattern to his environment, and 2) what are the affects on the self when African American men respond to imperceptible environmental stimuli?

Today African Americans are facing a resurgence of the climate that supported the mark of oppression just a short time ago. Negative images of African American men have resurfaced into profitable endeavors, thereby recreating an environment of unfavorable but positively framed racial images broadcast by two of the farthest reaching mediums: television and radio. Located within the glamour and popularity of Black entertainment, there exists the projection of a negative, although financially rewarded, Black image. Historically African American men have faced negative images as lazy, shiftless, and simple people. Currently these images take the form of modern day gangsters and oversexed men fulfilling a multitude of hedonistic desires. What is the problem? The problem is that the African American male environment that inherently involves the display of negative images of African American men now includes socially acceptable and profitable images of negative behavior that are considered to be the construct in describing the Black male. Young Black males have been duped into believing that the lyrics broadcast and visual images displayed on television through the overabundance of rap and video shows correspond to their true nature as African American men (Matthews, 2000). The adoption of these synthetic value sets form a posture within the psyche of African American males that possesses the potential to hamper their ability to develop healthy relationships with African American women, potentially add to the overpopulation of Black males in prison (currently numbering around one million), and decrease the college enrollment rates for African American men.

Matthews conceptualizes this thought (when referring to the impact of rap music on African American men) by stating, "We all need to get serious about helping these young people discern the inevitable consequences of hipping and hopping their opportunities away. Believe me if we don't, the unsavory pied pipers of hip hop will lead them to a place that none of us wants to see them go." The notion that African American males adopt artificially generated ideas to govern their sense of self carries with it a second hidden danger. As societal genres change, the individual who looks to societal mores for guidance must also change. If societal values conflict with individual, familial, or racial norms, the individual may find himself at the crossroads of skepticism and despondency. Many young African American males find themselves in this precarious position on a daily basis. They are unsure as to the direction of their lives and are additionally hesitant about choosing endeavors that are representative of foreign social and cultural beliefs. If this cloud of despair goes unrestricted, the second, and most dangerous, hidden snare will claim future generations of African American males.

Discussing nihilism as a pitfall facing African American men is a topic that connects with countless facets of the Black man's experience in America. In every dimension of African American life there stands an eternal struggle to determine for oneself the underpinnings of one's existence. Throughout the hundreds of years that African American men have existed in America, socioracial conditions have created an existential vacuum, a condition of emptiness and hollowness that result from meaninglessness in life, which has fueled the fires of nihilistic living for many of our young brothers.

Nihilism, as proposed by Albert Camus, is a problem of meaninglessness for each individual. Vincent Perez (2000), writing about nihilism and cultural memory in Chicano urban narratives, describes nihilism from the perspective of a race-based and punitive society that inexorably surrounds urban youth. This is an examination of nihilism as a position unconsciously assumed by African American males to the idea that all values and beliefs are enigmatic and worthless and, consequently, existence is artificial. This does not mean to presuppose that all African Americans possess a disposition of nihilism. Rather, the departure from previously held values by many African Americans is a result of nihilism. My experience as a Health and Human Service professional serving poor and working class African Americans in a large urban city will provide additional information to draw out my point.

To begin, many African Americans in our community may not know nor care about the term nihilism, although they may have experienced it and verbalize it, somewhat, on a daily basis. Perez conceptualizes this point by examining Richard Wright's (1998) text *Native Son* illustrating that nihilism in the mind of the urban African American is a cognizant response that manifests itself to oppose the inequitable socio-racial and political conditions inherent in the urban community. African American opposition to society can take the form of gangs, cessation of educational endeavors, and involvement in the use and/or distribution of illicit substances. The nature of our society, when applied to members of particular racial and economic groups, carries with it inequitable treatment. Social structure theorists have studied the manner of our society and the manner by which society creates the feeling of nihilism in minority and low income groups. Strain theorists posit a model of understanding the resulting oppositional behavior from individuals living at lower levels of the socioeconomic ladder. It does not contend that a person's socioeconomic status nor their value set motivates the manifestation of opposing behavior but it is the illegitimate denial of achieving like social and financial successes that. The strain that develops in the individual is the realization that the products and pleasures of life available to other members of society are personally out of reach. Therefore individuals affected through this process develop alternative means (gangs, illegitimate enterprise, etc) of acquiring the superfluity of American culture. The pitfall of nihilism, then, is in the period of time between the individual's recognition of strain and the chosen attitudinal and behavioral responses to that strain. At the point of recognizing the inauthenticity of societal values and the aspiration to abandon any continued adherence to them, the African American man will find himself in an extreme circumstance.

As a Health and Human Service professional, I have witnessed the emotional devastation and the resulting negative behavioral actions of African American men who have dismissed the morality of their environment because of the incongruence between explicit social messages (liberty and justice for all, fair and impartial jury, equal opportunity employer) and staunch reality.

Working with African American men and adolescents on issues ranging from recovery to interpersonal skills has revealed to me indispensable amounts of insight. I remember talking to a group of African American adolescent males ranging in age from 15 to 17 years of age. They were part of program designed to house young boys torn between leaving or returning their homes. I was asked to come into the program and attempt to motivate the youngsters to return home and re-engage in a society that has already demonstrated numerous inconsistencies regarding love, education, and opportunity. I remember one young man was a few months away from his eighteenth birthday.

Throughout our discussion, this young man consistently denied the attachment to any definable set of cultural, social, or ethnic values. He preferred to espouse his desire to participate in arbitrary local subculture rituals of hanging out late, skipping school, smoking blunts (cigars emptied of their tobacco and refilled with marijuana), drinking wine, and doing as little as possible. When asked the question, "do you see a change coming in your life?" he replied, "no." I called to his attention his impending birthday. I asked him does he see the significance of that day. The young man only replied that it is just another day. I answered him by saying, "for you that may be the case, but for the law it is not."

I wanted him to see that his reasoning of negating the values and beliefs of his home, community, and society thereby rendering them meaningless in his life did not remove the consequences that his behavioral responses would bring upon him under the auspices of being socially and legally defined as an adult.

It is in this state that African American men find themselves susceptible to the additional snares of our society such as contact with the justice system, missed educational and vocational opportunities, and susceptibility to drug addiction. Where nothingness exists, nothing matters. Whether it was my role as a social worker or as an outpatient therapist, I have personally witnessed the internal struggle that surrounds African American men caught in the snare of nothingness. The snare of nothingness creates uncertainty in the minds of African American males that unconsciously shapes their reactions to the world around them.

These reactions, however justified in the mind of the Black male, encounter a dominant culture primarily disconnected and largely unresponsive to the plight of persons living along the racial divide.

Dr. Cyrus M. Ellis is a twenty-year veteran of the United States Army serving on Active Duty, in the Army National Guard and the United States Army Reserve as an enlisted soldier and as an Army Officer in the United States Army Reserve.

He is a recipient of the Army Commendation Medal (x2), Army Achievement Medal (x3), Armed Forces Reserve Medal (w/M device), Army Reserve Achievement Medal (x2), Army Good Conduct Medal, & National Defense Medal.

He has held positions as a platoon leader, company commander and evaluation officer.

www.ingramcontent.com/pod-product-compliance
Lightning Source LLC
Chambersburg PA
CBHW022110160426
43198CB00008B/424